THE GAMBOLS

BOOK No 42

by Barry Appleby

Pedigree BOOKS

Published by Pedigree Books Limited
The Old Rectory, Matford Lane, Exeter, Devon, EX2 4PS.
Under licence from Express Newspapers plc.

£3.95

IF YOU'RE THINKING OF GIVING THIS BOOK AS A PRESENT TO A FRIEND, YOU CAN CUT OFF THE PRICE HERE

GA 42

I'M GOING TO SPRING CLEAN THE HOUSE TO-DAY

POOR GAYE... SHE'LL BE TIRED – I MUST GIVE HER SOME PRAISE TO CHEER HER UP....

DARLING IT ALL LOOKS **WONDERFUL**

I HAVEN'T DONE THIS ROOM YET

© 1993 Barry Appleby

1-3 5683

WHY DIDN'T YOU TELL THEM THAT WE'RE MARRIED?

PRIVATE PARTY

BECAUSE IT'D MAKE US SEEM SO OLD FASHIONED

ER.. YES.. I SUPPOSE IT WOULD

NEVERTHELESS I DO WISH YOU'D STOP INTRODUCING ME TO STRANGERS AS THE MAN YOU'RE LIVING WITH

BUT IT'S TRUE

© 1993 Barry Appleby

TUES 23-2 5678

WELL.. YES.. YES..!

© 1993 Barry Appleby

THAT'S A **VERY** GOOD SUGGESTION

I MUST CONFESS I'D **NEVER** HAVE THOUGHT OF THAT MYSELF

WELL.....DON'T SOUND SO SURPRISED

21-2

THERE'S **NOTHING** LIKE
A HEARTY BREAKFAST
TO START THE DAY

YOU REALLY DO HAVE TO DO YOUR
ACCOUNTS YOURSELF TO KNOW JUST
WHERE YOU STAND FINANCIALLY

GAYE IS QUITE SURE THAT EVERY SINGLE MOMENT SPENT LOOKING AFTER HER APPEARANCE IS VERY WORTH WHILE

OOH— JUST LOOK AT ME....

WHAT A MESS...
—MY HAIR—
NO MAKE·UP—
UNTIDY AND OLD

AH WELL— WHAT OF IT?

IT'S ONLY SEVEN A.M.

© 1993 Barry Appleby
5732 TUES

GAYE ALWAYS LIKES TRYING OUT NEW THINGS

NEW!
BEAUTY CREAM
SCIENTIFIC REVOLUTION

SURPRISE— SURPRISE·!!

DARLING!

IT'S ABSOLUTELY GUARANTEED TO IMPROVE YOUR APPEARANCE

ER...YOU THINK MY APPEARANCE WANTS IMPROVING?

YOU BEAST— I HATE YOU

© 1992 Barry Appleby
WED 5577

NOW LET'S GET THIS CLEAR...

YOU HAVEN'T ANY ROOM IN YOUR WARDROBE?

AND YOU HAVEN'T A THING TO WEAR?

NO

OOH! YOU MEN WILL NEVER UNDERSTAND WOMEN'S PROBLEMS

© 1992 Barry Appleby
5418

GAYE **LOVES** FINDING A BARGAIN—BUT DON'T WE ALL?

GEORGE'S IDEA OF A GOOD TAILOR
AND GAYE'S IDEA DON'T ALWAYS AGREE!

SUPERMARKETS ARE THE SAME ALL ROUND THE WORLD

© 1992 Barry Appleby FRI 11-12 5615

5435

GAYE IS THE FIRST TO ADMIT THAT SHE MUST BE MAD

POOR GEORGE – ALWAYS IN TROUBLE –
HAD A LITTLE SPELL IN HOSPITAL
LAST YEAR

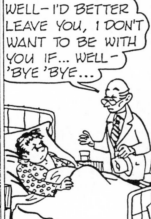

WE LOVE HAVING OUR NIECE & NEPHEW TO STAY WITH US — BUT OH DEAR THEY DO TAKE SOME KEEPING UP WITH —

WHY DO WOMEN ALWAYS CRY AT WEDDINGS—
—IT ISN'T AS IF THEY HAVE TO WEAR
THOSE AWFUL HIRE-SUITS

THERE ARE TIMES WHEN GAYE IS AWFULLY 'CATTY' ABOUT OTHER WOMEN—BUT SHE DOESN'T **REALLY** MEAN WHAT SHE SAYS

IF YOU ASK GEORGE IF HE'S IN LOVE — HE'D DITHER AND GO ALL EMBARRASSED AND LIKE ALL HUSBANDS — HE'D PROBABLY SAY "ER... YES ... I SUPPOSE SO..."

COOEE— I'M HOME

NO!

THAT'S BETTER

©1992 Barry Appleby
MON 5587

I'VE BEEN THINKING

OH?

D'YOU KNOW WHAT I LIKE BEST ABOUT YOU?

ER....NO

YOUR LAP'S SO NICE AND SOFT

©1992 Barry Appleby
8-11

DARLING!

HOW ROMANTIC

LATER

DAMN FOOL THING TO DO

5533

PERFUME
AROUSAL
NEW SEXY

GEORGE, DARLING, WHAT DO YOU THINK OF MY NEW PERFUME?

OH? IS THAT WHAT THE FUNNY SMELL IS

WELL— THAT WAS A WASTE OF MONEY

© 1992 Barry Appleby

THURS
5536

HAPPY WEDDING ANNIVERSARY DARLING

SAME TO YOU MY PET

OF ALL THE MEN IN THE WHOLE WORLD I CAN'T THINK OF A SINGLE ONE I'D HAVE SOONER MARRIED THAN GEORGE

PURRRRR

© 1992 Barry Appleby

WED 5553

GAYE LOVES HER PART TIME OFFICE JOB—
SHE FEELS THAT IT KEEPS HER UP
WITH ALL THE LATEST GOSSIP

WHEN POOR GAYE WAS FORBIDDEN
TO TALK — NOT EVEN IN A WHISPER —
SHE THOUGHT SHE'D GO BARMY

WEDNESDAY 26TH MAY 1993

THERE'S NOTHING LIKE A GOOD HOLIDAY
IN THE SUN — IT GIVES YOU THE STRENGTH
TO WORK HARD
AND EARN ENOUGH MONEY
TO AFFORD ANOTHER HOLIDAY
NEXT YEAR

GAYE WILL TELL YOU THAT THE ADVANTAGE OF A CORDLESS TELEPHONE IS THAT SHE CAN MAKE HER CALLS ANYWHERE IN THE HOUSE — ON THE OTHER HAND GEORGE WILL TELL YOU THAT THEY DON'T STOP HER MAKING 'PHONE CALLS WHEREVER SHE IS.

GEORGE—ARE YOU FREE FOR A ROUND OF GOLF?

ER... SORRY

CLICK

BUT I'VE PROMISED TO TAKE GAYE SHOPPING

WELL—MY BEST WISHES FOR A SPEEDY RECOVERY

SAT 5538
©1992 Barry Appleby

BRRRRR. BRRRRR

BRRRRR BRRRRR

BRRRRR BRRRRR

BRRRR BRR

BRRRRR BRRRRR

BRRRR BRRRR

BRRRRR BRRRR

YES—JUST A MINUTE —I'LL CALL HIM

WED 5589
©1992 Barry Appleby

AND THEN WHAT DO YOU THINK.. ER?

NO—I CAN'T TELL YOU NOW

THERE'S SOMEONE HERE WHO'S LISTENING TO EVERY WORD I'M SAYING

I AM NOT LISTENING TO EVERY WORD YOU'RE SAYING

©1992 Barry Appleby   15-11

THERE YOU ARE— IT WAS SIMPLE

WELL— HE WOULDN'T TAKE HIS MEDICINE FOR ME

HOW IN THE WORLD DID YOU MANAGE IT?

TOLD HIM IT WAS RADIO-ACTIVE

©1992 Bally Appleby
WED 30-12 5631

WOULD YOU LIKE BAKED BEANS OR FISH FOR YOUR TEA?

OH! BAKED BEANS PLEASE

BAKED BEANS

WHY DO YOU ALWAYS GO FOR BAKED BEANS?

BECAUSE THERE'S NO PROBLEM WITH THE BONES

29-12 TUES 5630
©1992 Bally Appleby

YOU BOUGHT ALL THOSE CREAM BUNS FOR THEIR TEA?

YES

BUT THEY'VE ONLY JUST FINISHED THE LOT YOU BOUGHT THIS MORNING

I KNOW

BUT FLIVVER PERSUADED ME TO BUY SOME MORE

WELL—ALL I CAN SAY IS THAT WHEN HE GROWS UP HE'S GOING TO MAKE A WONDERFUL SALESMAN

MON 11-1 5641

THE BEST PART OF DOING IT YOURSELF
IS ALL THE MONEY IT SAVES — ALWAYS
PROVIDED OF COURSE THAT YOU DON'T
HAVE TO DO IT TWICE!

MUST GET IT DONE IN TIME FOR EASTER

WELL—THAT'S AS FAR AS I CAN GO TO-DAY

I'LL FINISH IT NEXT WEEK-END... NOW REMEMBER...

... PROMISE NOT TO TOUCH ANYTHING

21-3

I HATE THESE MORNINGS WHEN WE OVERSLEEP

©1992 Barry Appleby 5431

I DON'T UNDERSTAND HOW THEY GET THIS BALANCE

RING THEM UP AND ASK

OH NO—I COULDN'T DO THAT

©1992 Barry Appleby

I'D FEEL SO DAFT TALKING TO A COMPUTER

5432

WE EACH CELEBRATE OUR
BIRTHDAY — ONLY ONE EACH YEAR
— SEEMS A PITY SOMEHOW

THE OLD CHRISTMAS TRADITIONS DIE HARD

I WONDER IF ANYBODY HAS EVER ADDED UP ALL THE HOURS OF HER LIFE THAT THE AVERAGE HOUSEWIFE SPENDS COOKING MEALS

COME AND GET IT

GEORGE—I'VE COOKED A VERY SPECIAL MEAL....

SO DO YOU THINK THAT BRAINY ECONOMIST'S FORECAST OF OUR FUTURE COULD WAIT FOR JUST ONE EVENING?

© 1992 Barry Appleby
5539

THE BEST PART OF THIS DISH IS THE VERY SPECIAL SAUCE

IT GIVES IT A SORT OF INDESCRIBABLE PIQUANT.....ER...

WHERE ARE YOU GOING?

TO FETCH SOME KETCHUP

© 1992 Barry Appleby
1-11

I'VE BURNT THE DINNER—CARELESS OF ME...

BUT I'VE BEEN CAGED UP IN THIS HOUSE ALL DAY

IF ONLY THERE WAS A WAY I COULD ESCAPE FROM THIS MONOTONY.. ...SOMETHING NEW.. DIFFERENT...

THAT'S WHAT I LIKE ABOUT YOU GEORGE—YOU CAN TAKE A HINT

© 1992 Barry Appleby
SAT
5598

NOW—FOR THE FORTY SECOND TIME IN
OUR LIVES WE COME TO THE END OF
YET ANOTHER GAMBOLS ANNUAL AND
VERY DIFFERENT IT LOOKS FROM THE FIRST

IT'S QUITE SURPRISING AT THE
NUMBER OF READERS WHO WRITE
TO TELL US THAT THEY STILL HAVE
EVERY COPY SINCE NUMBER ONE

©1993 Barry Appleby

ISBN 1 874507 147
Printed in Italy